A Little Indulgence

COFFEE

Printed in the United States of America
by G&R Publishing Co.

Distributed By:

507 Industrial Street
Waverly, IA 50677

ISBN-13: 978-1-56383-216-1
ISBN-10: 1-56383-216-X
Item #6202

C O F F E E

Ah, coffee. The word alone conjures up feelings of warmth and comfort. It can calm the nerves or sustain energy, soothe the body or jolt the weary to wake. Coffee can be known for its strength, flavor or sweetness. Or sought after for its roast, color or bean. Because of its versatility, coffee is the standard drink for people all over the world, and has become a staple in the American home and workplace. Coffee can be hot or cold, strong or mild, good or bad, expensive or cheap. Sipped from a delicate demitasse or downed in a Styrofoam cup. Enjoyed in the peaceful solitude of the home kitchen or ordered in the buzzed rush of the corner café.

The story of coffee commences with the bean – the small brown twin of a cherry, which begins its life surrounded by jasmine-scented blossoms and yellow-copper leaves. Throughout its existence the little bean has been the commodity of countries, the currency of nations, the addiction of loyal absorbents and the livelihood of millions. Each day, the beans are cultivated by the millions. Next, the beans are roasted for flavor and ground into fragrant bits. The coffee grounds are then brewed by one of the many techniques known to man and served in one of the hundreds of forms available. The possibility of the coffee bean, it seems, is endless. So pour a fresh cup and turn the page to explore the world of coffee…

THE COFFEE BEAN

The most widely known species of the coffee plant are Coffea Arabica and Coffea Canephora. The beans of the Arabica are known for their superior flavor, while the beans of the later are recognized for their higher caffeine content. Canephora, known as Robusta, thrives in environments where Arabica will not grow, thus leading to its use as an inexpensive substitute for Arabica.

COFFEA ARABICA

Coffea Arabica represent approximately 70 percent of the world's coffee production. Arabica trees are costly to cultivate, as the better plants are generally grown between 2,000 and 6,000 feet above sea level. Their environment must remain mild, neither too hot nor too cold. The plants prefer temperatures between 59 and 75 degrees and a rainfall of nearly 60 inches per year. Though the trees are somewhat hearty, a heavy frost will nearly wipe them out. Arabica trees require a lot of care and attention and are more disease prone than the Robusta variety. Compared to Robusta, the beans of the Arabica plants are lower in caffeine, flatter and more elongated.

There are several varieties of Coffea Arabica: Bourbon, Typica, Caturra, Mundo, Novo, Tico, San Ramon, Jamaican Blue Mountain.

COFFEA CANEPHORA

Though Coffea Canephora accounts for only about 30 percent of the world's coffee market, production of the variety is increasing. The only known variety of Canephora, the Robusta, produces beans that contain 50 to 60 percent more caffeine than Arabica varieties. Because of their bitter taste, Robusta beans are primarily used in blends and for instant coffees. Robusta trees are easier to cultivate because of their tendency to be more disease resistant and the ability to withstand warmer climates. The trees prefer temperatures between 75 and 85 degrees, enabling growth at lower altitudes than Arabica trees.

GINGERBREAD LATTE

Makes 1 serving

2 oz. strong brewed
  coffee or espresso
2 T. gingerbread flavored
  syrup
½ C. milk, steamed

2 T. whipped topping
Pinch of nutmeg
Pinch of cinnamon

In a large mug, combine strong brewed coffee and gingerbread syrup. Pour steamed milk over coffee mixture. Mix well and top with whipped topping and sprinkle with nutmeg and cinnamon for garnish.

CHOCOLATE BUZZ
Makes 2 servings

1 C. milk
5 ice cubes
1 oz. strong brewed
  coffee or espresso

¾ C. chocolate ice cream
2 tsp. instant hot cocoa mix
2 T. chocolate syrup

In a blender, combine milk, ice cubes and brewed coffee or espresso. Process on high until smooth and add chocolate ice cream. Process until well blended and stir in hot cocoa mix and chocolate syrup. Pour mixture into two tall glasses and serve immediately.

SUNDAE COFFEES
Makes 6 servings

1 pint French vanilla
  ice cream

12 oz. Irish cream liqueur
12 C. hot brewed coffee

Fill each of 12 large mugs with a scoop of French vanilla
ice cream. Pour 1 ounce Irish cream liqueur over ice cream
in each mug. Pour hot brewed coffee over ice cream to fill
each mug. Serve immediately.

ICED WHITE COFFEE

Makes 8 servings

1½ qts. brewed coffee,
   room temperature
1 C. milk
1 C. half n' half

⅓ C. sugar
1 tsp. vanilla
2 T. crème de cacao liqueur

In a tall pitcher, combine cooled coffee, milk and half n' half. Mix well and stir in sugar, vanilla and crème de cacao. To serve, pour mixture over ice in glasses.

CINNAMON HAZELNUT COFFEE

Makes 2 servings

2 C. hot brewed coffee
¼ C. hazelnut flavored
  creamer
⅛ tsp. cinnamon

2 tsp. sugar
Whipped topping, optional

In a tall pitcher, combine coffee, hazelnut creamer, cinnamon and sugar. Stir until well mixed. Pour mixture into 2 large mugs and, if desired, top each serving with whipped topping. Serve immediately.

"Good communication is as stimulating as black coffee and just as hard to sleep after.

Anne Morrow Lindbergh

COFFEE LEGENDS

Many botanists believe coffee originated in Ethiopia as a food, rather than a beverage. Most often, the Arabs are credited with being the first to boil the raw seeds of the coffee plant with water to make a hot drink. Over the centuries, the myths and mysteries of the origin of coffee have become so great that the true invention of the beverage it is still uncertain.

Some historians trace the coffee bean back to the Old Testament, claiming it was the same "parched corn" that Abigail gave to David and Boaz gave to Ruth.

THE DANCING GOATS

Banesius, a late 18th-century writer, recounts, in a treatise he wrote on coffee, the fable of the famous dancing goats – the flock of an Ethiopian goat herder. The shepherd complained to the leader, the Imam, of a neighboring mon-astery that his herd "two or three times a week not only kept awake all night long but spent it frisking and dancing in an unusual manner."

The Imam went to the pasture where the goats danced and, upon finding berries growing on shrubs they had eaten from, decided to try them himself. He boiled the berries in water and drank the brew. When he was able to stay awake all night without any ill effects, the Imam "enjoin'd the daily use of it to his monks, which, by keeping them from sleep, made them more readily and surely attend the devotions they were obliged to perform at night time."

CHILLED MOCHA FUSION
Makes 1 serving

¾ C. milk
1 tsp. vanilla
3 T. sugar

3 T. mocha flavored instant coffee mix
1 C. ice cubes

In a blender, combine milk, vanilla, sugar, mocha coffee mix and ice. Blend until ice is crushed and mixture is smooth. Pour into a tall glass and serve immediately.

CALYPSO COFFEE
Makes 1 serving

1 oz. rum
1 oz. crème de cacao
  liqueur

1 C. hot brewed coffee
Whipped topping, optional

In a large mug, place rum and crème de cacao liqueur. Mix lightly and pour hot brewed coffee to fill mug. If desired, garnish with a dollop of whipped topping.

CAFÉ YOGURT

Makes 2 servings

1½ C. strong brewed
   coffee, cold
1½ C. plain yogurt

4 tsp. sugar
Pinch of cinnamon

In a blender, combine cold brewed coffee, plain yogurt and sugar. Process on high for 10 to 15 seconds, until well blended. Pour mixture into two tall glasses and garnish each serving with a sprinkle of cinnamon.

GROG

Makes 6 servings

Peel of 1 orange, broken
   into 6 pieces
Peel of 1 lemon, broken
   into 6 pieces
2 T. butter, softened
1 C. brown sugar

¼ tsp. ground cloves
¼ tsp. nutmeg
¼ tsp. cinnamon
3 C. hot brewed coffee
½ C. heavy whipping cream

Into each of six large mugs, place one piece of orange peel and one piece of lemon peel. In a small bowl, combine softened butter, brown sugar, ground cloves, nutmeg and cinnamon. In a large measuring cup, combine brewed coffee and heavy cream, mixing until well combined. Divide the butter mixture evenly into the six mugs and pour the hot coffee mixture evenly into each mug. Stir lightly and serve immediately.

" *To drink is human,*
to drink coffee is divine! "

Author Unknown

HOMEMADE COFFEE LIQUEUR
Makes 3 cups

2 C. water
1¼ C. sugar
2 T. vanilla

2 T. fresh ground coffee
   beans
2½ C. vodka

In a medium saucepan over medium heat, combine water, sugar, vanilla and fresh ground coffee beans. Bring mixture to a boil, reduce heat and let simmer for 10 minutes, stirring occasionally. Remove from heat and let cool. Pour mixture through a fine-hole sieve into a jar to strain out any coffee bits. When mixture has cooled, stir in vodka and funnel mixture into a bottle. Close bottle and store liqueur in a cool place for 2 to 4 weeks. Shake well before using.

SWEET HONEY LATTE

Makes 2 servings

1 C. hot milk
½ C. hot water
2½ tsp. instant coffee granules

1 T. honey
2 T. foamed milk, optional

In a blender, combine hot milk, hot water, instant coffee granules and honey. Process on high for 10 to 15 seconds, until well blended. Pour mixture into a mug and, if desired, top with foamed milk. Serve immediately.

COLD CAFÉ LATTE

Makes 4 servings

2 T. instant coffee granules
¾ C. warm water
1 (14 oz.) can sweetened
  condensed milk

1 tsp. vanilla
4 C. ice cubes

In a tall pitcher, dissolve instant coffee granules in warm water. Add sweetened condensed milk and vanilla. Stir until well combined. Divide ice cubes evenly into 4 tall glasses. Pour mixture over ice in each glass and serve immediately.

HOW DOES YOUR GARDEN GROW?

Humans are not the only ones who enjoy the benefits of coffee. Because of their high nitrogen content, brewed coffee grounds make great fertilizer for plants. Besides nitrogen, coffee grounds contain potassium, phosphorus and many other elements aiding in plant development. Roses, particularly, thrive when "fed" coffee grounds, becoming bigger and more colorful. Spent coffee grounds also help decompose a compost pile very rapidly.

COFFEE FERTILIZER

Try these simple tricks the next time you wish to fertilize your plants at home.

- Line a 9 x 13″ metal baking dish with newspaper. Spread the spent coffee grounds in an even layer, no more than ¼″ thick, over the dish. Let the grounds air dry. Once dried, work the grounds into the soil around your outdoor plants. For indoor, or container plants, simply sprinkle the dried grounds over the surface of the soil.

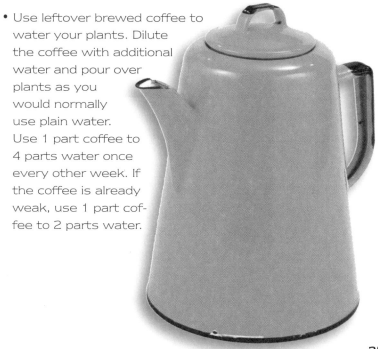

- Use leftover brewed coffee to water your plants. Dilute the coffee with additional water and pour over plants as you would normally use plain water. Use 1 part coffee to 4 parts water once every other week. If the coffee is already weak, use 1 part coffee to 2 parts water.

FIRESIDE COFFEE
Makes about 20 servings

½ C. powdered creamer
½ C. instant hot cocoa mix
½ C. instant coffee granules

¼ tsp. cinnamon
$1/8$ tsp. nutmeg

Into a large bowl, sift powdered creamer, instant hot cocoa and instant coffee granules. Add cinnamon and nutmeg. Stir until well combined. To prepare 1 coffee drink, add about 1 tablespoon mixture to 1 cup hot water. Stir until mixture is dissolved and serve immediately.

SPICED BREW
Makes 2 servings

2 T. ground coffee beans
¼ tsp. ground cardamom

2 T. sweetened
  condensed milk

In the filter of a coffee machine, place ground coffee beans and ground cardamom. Place enough water in the machine to make 2 cups. Prepare machine to brew coffee. Pour coffee evenly into two mugs and stir 1 tablespoon sweetened condensed milk into each mug. Serve immediately.

MOCHA CAFÉ MUDSLIDE
Makes 2 servings

1 C. mocha flavored creamer
4 tsp. instant coffee granules

2¼ C. ice cubes
2½ C. vanilla ice cream

In a blender, combine mocha flavored creamer and instant coffee granules. Process on high until coffee granules are completely dissolved. Add ice cubes and vanilla ice cream and process until mixture is smooth. Pour mixture evenly into two tall glasses and serve immediately.

PEPPERMINT CAPPUCCINO

Makes 1 serving

1 (1½˝) York peppermint
  patty, unwrapped
2 tsp. milk

1 C. hot brewed coffee
Whipped topping, optional

Cut peppermint patty into quarters. In a large mug, place peppermint patty pieces and milk. Microwave on high for 30 seconds. Remove from microwave and stir until chocolate from peppermint is melted. Pour hot coffee over melted chocolate and stir until chocolate is completely dissolved. If desired, top with whipped topping. Serve immediately.

JAVA BAHAMA MAMA

Makes 1 serving

¼ oz. coffee flavored liqueur   Juice of ½ lemon
¾ oz. dark rum   4 oz. pineapple juice
½ oz. coconut liqueur   1 maraschino cherry

In a cocktail shaker filled with ice, place coffee liqueur, rum, coconut liqueur, lemon juice and pineapple juice. Shake vigorously and strain mixture into a tall glass filled with ice. Garnish with a cherry.

MOCHA MARTINI
Makes 1 serving

1 (1½ oz.) jigger chocolate
  flavored liqueur
1 (1½ oz.) jigger rum
  flavored coffee liqueur

1 (1½ oz.) jigger vodka
1 maraschino cherry

In a cocktail shaker filled with ice, place chocolate flavored liqueur, rum flavored coffee liqueur and vodka. Shake vigorously and strain mixture into a martini glass. Garnish with a cherry.

FROM SEED TO CUP IN 10 STEPS

ONE – PLANTING

If a coffee bean is not dried, roasted and ground, it can be planted and will grow into a coffee tree. The seeds are typically planted in large beds in shaded nurseries. When the seedlings sprout, they are planted in individual pots of treated soil. They are shaded from bright sunlight and watered frequently, until they are strong enough to be permanently planted in the ground.

TWO – CHERRY HARVESTING

It will take approximately three to four years for a typical newly planted coffee tree to begin bearing fruit. The fruit of the coffee tree is a cherry, which turns bright deep red when ripe. The cherries are then picked by hand or machine. A good hand picker will harvest approximately 100 to 200 pounds of coffee cherries per day. This amount of cherries will produce 20 to 40 pounds of coffee beans. Approximately 4,000 beans are needed to produce one pound of roasted coffee. Few commodities require so much in terms of human effort!

THREE – PROCESSING

Processing the coffee cherries must begin as quickly as possible after the harvest, to prevent spoilage. The cherries are either processed by a dry or wet method. During the dry method, the fresh cherries are spread out on flat surfaces to dry in the sun. The cherries are raked and turned throughout the day and covered at night. This process continues (sometimes for several weeks) until the moisture content of the cherry drops to 11 percent.

The wet method is a little more involved, with the fresh cherries first passing through a pulping machine. The beans are sent through water channels and separated by weight, with the lighter beans floating to the top and the heavier, ripe beans sinking to the bottom. The beans are then divided by size and fermented in tanks for up to 48 hours. Finally, the beans are rinsed and ready to dry.

FOUR – DRYING THE BEANS

Beans that have been processed by wet method need to be dried. The beans are either dried in the sun or machine dried in large tumblers until their moisture content reaches 11 percent. Sun-dried beans are spread on flat tables and turned frequently.

FIVE – MILLING THE BEANS

Before exporting, the beans need to be hulled, polished, graded and sorted. Hulling the beans means removing the parchment layer, or the entire dried husk, to reveal the two beans inside each cherry. The beans may then be polished to remove any skin remaining on the beans. Then, the beans are precisely sorted by size and weight. It is also at this step that the beans are evaluated for color flaws or other imperfections. In many countries, the beans are sorted by hand, insuring that only the finest quality beans are exported.

SIX – EXPORTING

Milled beans are referred to as 'green coffee.' The green coffee is bagged and then loaded into shipping containers. The containers are placed on ships ready to transport around the world. Approximately seven million tons of green coffee are produced worldwide each year.

SEVEN – TASTING

Throughout every stage of its production, coffee is tasted for quality. The taster, also known as the cupper, first evaluates the beans for appearance. The beans are then roasted, immediately ground and infused in boiling water by a carefully controlled method. The cupper evaluates the brew for aroma, weight and taste. An expert cupper can denote the subtle differences between batches of coffee beans, even after hundreds of samples each day.

EIGHT – ROASTING

Green coffee is transformed through the roasting process into the aromatic brown beans we purchase in stores. The beans are moved throughout a roasting machine, which maintains a temperature of about 550 degrees. When the beans reach an internal temperature of 400 degrees, they begin to turn brown and the oil locked inside each bean begins to emerge. The beans are then removed from the roaster and immediately cooled. Generally, roasting is performed in the importing country, since fresh roasted beans must ideally reach the consumer as quickly as possible.

NINE – GRINDING

Coffee beans are ground to release the most amount of flavor contained inside each bean. The finer the grind, the more quickly the coffee should be prepared. Espresso machines, for example, require a much finer ground coffee than that which will be brewed in a drip system.

TEN – BREWING

Brewing coffee is the method of mixing dry coffee beans or coffee grounds with water. The brewing process can be achieved by one of many methods, ranging from very simple techniques to the use of expensive complex machines. Brewing the perfect cup of coffee depends on many factors, including the grind of the beans, the condition and temperature of the water, the ratio of coffee to water and the contact time between the two ingredients. So the next time you sit down to enjoy a warm cup of this aromatic beverage, take a moment to appreciate the long voyage the beans have traveled to be in your cup of coffee.

FRENCH VANILLA MOCHA

Makes 1 serving

¾ C. hot water
1 T. instant coffee granules
¼ C. French vanilla flavored
  creamer

1 T. chocolate syrup
Whipped topping, optional

In a large mug, combine hot water and instant coffee granules. Mix well, until coffee granules are completely dissolved. Stir in French vanilla creamer and chocolate syrup. If desired, top with whipped topping.

VANILLA COFFEE KISS

Makes 2 servings

½ C. hot brewed coffee
½ C. French vanilla flavored
  creamer

1 T. cocoa powder
Whipped topping, optional

In a tall pitcher, combine coffee, French vanilla creamer and cocoa powder. Stir until well mixed. Pour mixture into 2 large mugs and, if desired, top each serving with whipped topping. Serve immediately.

CAFÉ MUDSLIDE
Makes 2 servings

1 C. French vanilla
 flavored creamer
4 tsp. instant coffee granules

2¼ C. ice cubes
2½ C. vanilla ice cream

In a blender, combine French vanilla creamer and instant coffee granules. Process on high until coffee granules are completely dissolved. Add ice cubes and vanilla ice cream and process until mixture is smooth. Pour mixture evenly into two tall glasses and serve immediately.

ORIGINAL IRISH COFFEE
Makes 1 serving

1 (1½ oz.) jigger Irish
 cream liqueur
1 (1½ oz.) jigger Irish whiskey

1 C. hot brewed coffee
1 T. whipped topping
Dash of nutmeg

In a large mug, combine Irish cream liqueur and Irish whiskey. Fill mug with hot coffee and mix lightly. Top with whipped topping and garnish with a dash of nutmeg. Serve immediately.

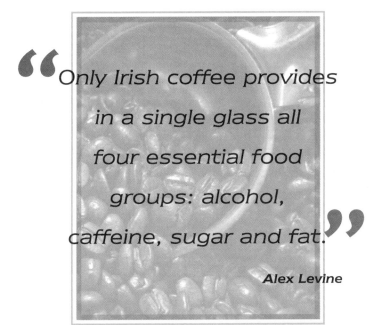

"*Only Irish coffee provides in a single glass all four essential food groups: alcohol, caffeine, sugar and fat.*"

Alex Levine

COFFEE PRODUCING COUNTRIES & TERRITORIES

AFRICA

Angola, Benin, Burundi, Cameroon, Cape Verde, Central African Republic, Comoros, Congo, Democratic Republic of Congo, Equatorial Guinea, Ethiopia, Gabon, Ghana, Guinea, Cote d'Ivoire, Kenya, Liberia, Madagascar, Malawi, Mozambique, Nigeria, Reunion, Rwanda, St. Helena, Sao Tome & Principe, Sierra Leone, South Africa, Sudan, Tanzania, Togo, Uganda, Zambia, Zimbabwe

CENTRAL AMERICA & CARIBBEAN

Costa Rice, Cuba, Dominican Republic, El Salvador, Guadeloupe, Guatemala, Haiti, Honduras, Jamaica, Martinique, Mexico, Nicaragua, Panama, Puerto Rico, Trinidad & Tobago

SOUTH AMERICA

Argentina, Bolivia, Brazil, Colombia, Ecuador, French Guiana, Galapagos Islands, Guyana, Paraguay, Peru, Suriname, Venezuela

SOUTH PACIFIC & SOUTHEAST ASIA

Australia, Cambodia, China, Fiji, French Polynesia, Hawaii, India, Indonesia, Laos, Malaysia, New Caledonia, Papua New Guinea, Philippines, Sri Lanka, Taiwan, Thailand, Vanuatu, Vietnam

JAMAICA COFFEE
Makes 1 serving

¾ oz. dark rum
¾ oz. coffee flavored liqueur
1 C. brewed coffee

2 T. whipped topping
1 chocolate covered
  coffee bean

In a large mug, place dark rum and coffee liqueur. Add hot coffee and stir slightly. Top with whipped topping and garnish with chocolate covered coffee bean. Serve immediately.

QUICK CAFÉ BROWNIES
Makes 12 servings

1 C. chocolate chips
¼ C. butter
1 T. instant coffee granules
1 egg
1 egg yolk
⅔ C. flour

½ C. sugar
⅛ tsp. baking soda
1 T. coffee flavored liqueur
1 tsp. vanilla
⅓ C. powdered sugar

Preheat oven to 350°. In an 8″ square baking dish, place chocolate chips and butter. Place baking dish over medium heat on stovetop and stir until mixture is melted. Remove from heat and stir in instant coffee granules, egg and egg yolk, mixing well. Into a medium bowl, sift flour, sugar and baking soda. Fold sifted mixture into chocolate mixture. Mix in coffee liqueur and vanilla, spreading mixture evenly in pan. Bake in oven for 20 to 25 minutes. Remove from oven and let cool. Before serving, sift powdered sugar over brownies and cut into squares.

PUDDING MOCHA PIE
Makes 1 (9˝) pie

1 (3½ oz.) pkg. non-instant
  chocolate pudding mix
2 C. milk
2 tsp. instant coffee granules
2 T. sugar

1 (9˝) prepared chocolate
  cookie crumb crust
3 C. whipped topping
½ tsp. vanilla

Prepare chocolate pudding according to package directions, using the 2 cups milk. In a medium bowl, combine 1 cup prepared chocolate pudding, instant coffee granules and sugar. Stir until sugar is dissolved and chill in refrigerator. Chill remaining pudding for 5 minutes, stirring occasionally and pour into prepared crust. Chill in refrigerator. Remove the chilled pudding and coffee mixture from the refrigerator and beat well. Blend whipped topping into coffee mixture. Spread coffee mixture evenly over pudding in crust. Chill for several hours before serving.

SPICED COFFEE BREAD
Makes 1 (9˝) loaf

1 C. hot brewed coffee
½ C. raisins
½ C. shortening
1 C. sugar
2 eggs
2 T. molasses
1 tsp. vanilla
1 tsp. cinnamon

½ tsp. nutmeg
½ tsp. ground cloves
½ tsp. ground ginger
2 C. flour
1 tsp. baking soda
½ tsp. salt
½ C. chopped walnuts

Preheat oven to 350°. In a small bowl, place brewed coffee and raisins and set aside until raisins are plump. Do not drain the bowl. In a medium bowl, combine shortening, sugar and eggs, mixing until well creamed, and add molasses and vanilla. In a separate bowl, combine cinnamon, nutmeg, cloves, ginger, flour, baking soda and salt. Make a well in the center of the dry ingredients and pour creamed mixture into the middle. Mix well and fold in coffee and raisin mixture and chopped walnuts. Pour batter into a greased 5 x 9˝ loaf pan and bake in oven for 1 hour.

COFFEE AS MEDICINE

About a thousand years ago, coffee was known as a medicine. Rhazes (850-922 AD), a Persian Iraq doctor and follower of Galen and Hippocrates, compiled a medical encyclopedia in which he notes the healing properties of the coffee plant. Similar references to coffee as a medicine appear in the writings of Avicenna (980-1037 AD), a distinguished Muslim physician and philosopher. Many of coffee's initial uses were to treat physical ailments, such as kidney stones, gout, smallpox, measles and coughs.

"O COFFEE! thou dispellest the cares of the great: thou bringest back those who wander from the paths of knowledge. Coffee is the beverage of the people of God, and the cordial of his servants who thirst for wisdom..."

From the Transylvania Journal of Medicine in the early 19th century. Believed to be the original work of Sheik Abdal-Kader Anasari Djezeri Haubuli, son of Mohammed.

COFFEE IN RELIGION

Mufti of Aden, a respected authority on Muslim law, and his monks took to drinking coffee in the mosque. Soon, religious communities throughout Arabia followed suit by taking up coffee drinking. In a ceremonious manner, coffee was served in mosques with a background of spiritual chanting. Drinking the warm, strong coffee was seen as a wholesome and virtuous activity. After the monks had their fill, the Imam would offer coffee to other worshippers present in the mosque.

PECAN MOCHA DELIGHT
Makes 1 (9″) cake

½ C. butter
8 (1 oz.) squares semi-
sweet chocolate, divided
3 eggs
¾ C. sugar
1¼ C. finely ground pecans

2 T. flour
5 T. coffee flavored liqueur,
divided
1 tsp. vanilla
1 T. powdered sugar

Preheat oven to 325°. In a medium saucepan over medium heat, combine butter and 6 squares semisweet chocolate. Heat, stirring frequently, until mixture is melted and smooth. In a large mixing bowl, beat eggs and sugar at high speed for 3 minutes, until mixture is thickened. Stir in ground pecans and flour. Add 3 tablespoons coffee liqueur and vanilla to the melted chocolate mixture. Add chocolate mixture to batter, mixing until well combined. Pour batter into a greased 9″ springform pan. Bake in oven for 35 to 45 minutes, or until a toothpick inserted in center of cake comes out clean. Remove from oven and let cool in pan. Remove cake from pan and place on a serving platter. In a microwave-safe bowl, combine remaining 2 squares chocolate and remaining 2 tablespoons coffee liqueur. Heat in microwave, stirring occasionally, until mixture is melted and smooth. Sift powdered sugar over top of cake and drizzle with melted chocolate mixture.

CRÈME BRULEE
Makes 6 individual servings

2 C. vanilla nut flavored
   creamer
½ C. milk
3 T. instant coffee granules

2 T. sugar
3 large eggs
3 large egg yolks
¼ C. brown sugar

Preheat oven to 300°. In a medium saucepan over medium heat, combine vanilla nut flavored creamer, milk, instant coffee granules and sugar. Heat, stirring frequently, until coffee is completely dissolved, being careful not to boil. Remove from heat. In a medium bowl, whisk together eggs and egg yolks. Gradually add egg mixture to creamer mixture, mixing with a wire whisk. Pour mixture evenly into six 4 ounce ramekins. Place ramekins on a jellyroll pan and fill jellyroll pan with 1″ hot water. Bake in oven for 40 to 45 minutes, or until center of custards are set. Remove ramekins from jellyroll pan and let cool on a wire rack for 1 hour. Sprinkle tops of custards with brown sugar and place under broiler for 1 to 2 minutes, until sugar begins to melt. Place in refrigerator until ready to serve.

"*If it wasn't for coffee, I'd have no discernible personality at all.*"

David Letterman

"*As soon as coffee is in your stomach, there is a general commotion. Ideas begin to move... similes arise, the paper is covered. Coffee is your ally and writing ceases to be a struggle.*"

Honoré de Balzac

THE FIRST COFFEEHOUSE

Over time, coffee began to lose its religious associations and coffee houses emerged throughout the Middle East in the early 16th century. Drinking coffee at home became popular around the same time. Coffee drinking happened everywhere and no social interaction was complete without it. Coffee was served at the barbershop, by merchants, to welcome guests and friends to the home and at formal banquets. With so many coffee houses springing up, competition for customers became fierce. Coffee house masters would attract customers with entertainment and lavish decorations. Within these coffee houses, one could find musicians, dancers, poets, card games and chess, among other amusements.

CAPPUCCINO CHEESECAKE
Makes 1 (9″) cake

1¾ C. crushed chocolate
  wafer cookies
½ C. sugar, divided
⅓ C. butter, melted
3 (8 oz.) pkgs. cream
  cheese, softened
1 C. French vanilla flavored
  creamer

4 large eggs
6 tsp. instant coffee
  granules
¼ C. flour
¾ C. white baking chips
1 (16 oz.) container sour
  cream, room temperature

Preheat oven to 350°. In a small bowl, combine chocolate wafer cookie crumbs and ¼ cup sugar. Stir in melted butter and press mixture into bottom and 1″ up sides of an ungreased 9″ springform pan. Bake in oven for 5 minutes. In a large mixing bowl, beat together cream cheese and French vanilla creamer at medium speed, until well combined. In a medium bowl, beat together eggs and instant coffee granules, mixing until coffee granules are completely dissolved. Add egg mixture, flour and remaining

¼ cup sugar to cream cheese mixture and mix well. Pour mixture over crust in pan. Return to oven for an additional 45 to 50 minutes, until edges are set but center of cheesecake moves slightly. In a microwave-safe bowl, heat white baking chips in microwave for 1 minute. Stir and return to microwave for 10 second intervals until white chocolate is melted and smooth. Stir in sour cream and spread mixture over cheesecake. Return to oven for an additional 10 minutes. Remove from oven and let cool on a wire rack. Refrigerate for several hours or overnight before serving.

BLACK RUSSIAN CAKE
Makes 1 bundt cake

1 (18¼ oz.) pkg. yellow
cake mix
1 (6 oz.) pkg. instant
chocolate pudding mix
4 eggs
½ C. sugar
1 C. vegetable oil

¼ C. vodka
½ C. coffee flavored
liqueur, divided
¾ C. water
1 C. powdered sugar,
divided

Preheat oven to 350°. Grease and flour a bundt cake pan. In a large mixing bowl, combine cake mix, chocolate pudding mix, eggs, sugar, vegetable oil, vodka, ¼ cup coffee liqueur and water. Beat at high speed for 4 minutes and pour batter into prepared pan. Bake in oven for 40 minutes. Remove from oven and let cool. Meanwhile, to prepare glaze, in a medium bowl, combine ½ cup powdered sugar and remaining ¼ cup coffee liqueur. Invert cake onto a serving platter and poke holes in surface of cake with a fork. Drizzle glaze over top of cake, letting glaze run down sides of cake. Sift remaining ½ cup powdered sugar over cake.

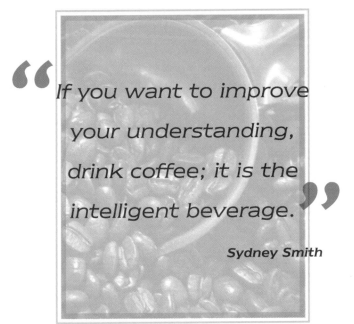

" If you want to improve your understanding, drink coffee; it is the intelligent beverage. "

Sydney Smith

DREAMY MOCHA CAKE
Makes 1 (9″) cake

1½ C. hot water
2 T. instant coffee granules, divided
1 C. powdered creamer
2⅓ C. flour, divided
1½ tsp. baking soda
2 C. white baking chips, divided
⅓ C. vegetable oil
1⅔ C. sugar

4 large eggs
⅔ C. evaporated milk
2 T. white vinegar
1 tsp. vanilla
⅔ C. cocoa powder
⅓ C. butter
2 (3 oz.) pkgs. cream cheese, softened
4 C. powdered sugar

Preheat oven to 350°. Grease and lightly flour two 9″ round cake pans. In a medium bowl, combine hot water and 1 tablespoon instant coffee granules. Using a wire whisk, stir in powdered creamer. In a separate bowl, combine 1⅔ cups flour and baking soda. In a microwave-safe bowl, combine 1⅓ cups white baking chips and vegetable oil. Microwave on high for 1 minute. Remove and stir in coffee mixture, sugar, eggs, evaporated milk, vinegar and vanilla, mixing with a wire whisk. Gradually add mixture to flour mixture. Pour 3¼ cups of the batter in a separate bowl and fold in remaining ⅔ cups flour. Pour mixture evenly into prepared pans. Add cocoa powder to remaining batter and slowly pour cocoa batter into the center of the batter in each pan. Bake in oven for 40 to 45 minutes, or until a toothpick inserted in center of cakes comes out clean. Remove from oven and let cool. Meanwhile, to prepare frosting, in a microwave-safe bowl, combine butter and remaining ⅔ cup white baking chips. Microwave on high until chocolate is almost melted. In a small bowl, combine remaining 1 tablespoon instant coffee granules and 1½ teaspoons water. Stir coffee mixture and cream cheese into white chocolate. Gradually fold in powdered sugar until frosting reaches desired consistency. To assemble cake, place one cake layer on a serving platter and top with some of the frosting. Place other cake layer on top and frost top and sides of cake.

LAYERED TIRAMISU CAKE

Makes 1 (9″) cake

1 (18¼ oz.) pkg. white
cake mix
1 tsp. instant coffee granules
¼ C. brewed coffee
5 T. coffee flavored liqueur,
divided
1 (8 oz.) pkg. mascarpone
cheese

¾ C. powdered sugar,
divided
2 C. heavy whipping cream
2 T. cocoa powder
1 (1 oz.) square semisweet
chocolate

Preheat oven to 350°. Grease and lightly flour three 9″ round
cake pans. In a large bowl, prepare cake mix according
to package directions. Divide the cake batter evenly into
three parts. Pour two of the parts into two of the prepared
cake pans. Add 1 teaspoon instant coffee granules to the
remaining batter and pour into the remaining pan. Bake in
oven for 20 to 25 minutes, or until a toothpick inserted in
center of cakes comes out clean. Remove from oven and
let cool for 10 minutes. Meanwhile, in a measuring cup,

combine brewed coffee and 1 tablespoon coffee liqueur and set aside. To prepare filling, in a small mixing bowl, combine mascarpone, ½ cup powdered sugar and 2 tablespoons coffee liqueur at low speed just until smooth. Cover and refrigerate. To prepare frosting, in a medium mixing bowl, beat heavy cream, remaining ¼ cup powdered sugar and remaining 2 tablespoons coffee liqueur and beat at medium high speed until stiff. Fold half of the cream mixture into the filling mixture. To assemble cake, place one cake layer on a serving platter and poke holes on the surface of the cake. Pour ⅓ of the coffee mixture over cake and top with half of the filling mixture. Top with coffee flavored cake layer, poke holes in cake and pour another ⅓ of the coffee mixture over layer. Top with remaining filling. Top with final cake layer, poke holes and pour remaining coffee layer over cake. Spread frosting over top and sides of cake. Lightly dust top of cake with cocoa powder and garnish with curls of chocolate. Refrigerate for 30 minutes before serving.

COFFEE ICE CREAM PIE
Makes 1 (9") pie

1⅛ C. crushed chocolate
wafer cookies

½ C. plus 1 T. butter,
melted, divided

10 T. coffee flavored liqueur,
divided

1 tsp. instant coffee or
espresso granules

3 oz. semisweet chocolate,
chopped

1 pint vanilla ice cream,
softened

1 pint chocolate ice cream,
softened

Whipped topping

Preheat oven to 325°. In a medium bowl, combine crushed chocolate cookies and ½ cup melted butter. Mix well and press mixture into bottom and up sides of a 9″ pie plate. Bake in oven for 10 minutes. Remove from oven and let cool completely. In a small saucepan over low heat, combine 6 tablespoons coffee liqueur and instant coffee granules. Heat, stirring frequently, until coffee granules are completely dissolved. Stir in chopped chocolate and remaining 1 tablespoon melted butter. Remove from heat and let cool. In a medium mixing bowl, place vanilla ice cream and 2 tablespoons coffee liqueur. Beat at low speed until well blended. Spread ice cream mixture over cooled crust in pie pan. Top with cooled chocolate mixture, spreading evenly. Place pie in freezer until firm. When firm, in a medium mixing bowl, beat together chocolate ice cream and remaining 2 tablespoons coffee liqueur. Beat at low speed until well blended and spread over pie. Return to freezer until firm. Before serving, top with dollops of whipped topping. Store leftovers in freezer.

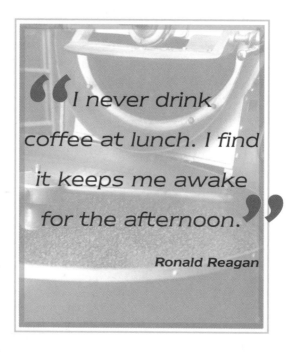

"I never drink coffee at lunch. I find it keeps me awake for the afternoon."

Ronald Reagan

CAFFEINE PLEASE

Coffee beans and brewed coffee contain caffeine, which acts as a stimulant. Coffee is often consumed when the drinker needs a "jolt" of energy, such as in the morning or during working hours. Coffee breaks are often taken throughout the day to restore liveliness and students preparing for exams have been known to down cup after cup of the hot drink. Researchers have also discovered an unknown chemical within coffee, which stimulates the production of cortisone and adrenaline, two stimulating hormones.

I'LL TAKE DECAF

Decaffeinated coffee is coffee from which most of the caffeine has been removed. Raw beans are soaked to absorb most of the caffeine, or a chemical solvent, such as trichloroethylene, is often used to remove the stimulant. Infused beverages that resemble coffee are also available and contain no caffeine.

BENEFITS OF
DRINKING COFFEE

Caffeinated coffee drinking has been known to
- increase the effectiveness of pain killers
- rid some people of asthma
- prevent gallstones and gallbladder disease in men
- reduce the risk of diabetes
- prevent colon and bladder cancers
- minimize the risk of hepatocellular carcinoma
- lower incidences of heart disease
- reduce the threat of liver cirrhosis
- increase short term memory and increase IQ
- help avoid muscle fatigue
- allow the body to burn a higher proportion of lipids
  to carbohydrates

AND THE RISKS

Caffeinated coffee drinkers have also been known to suffer from

- insomnia
- anxiety and irritability
- increased blood pressure among those with high blood pressure
- "coffee jitters" as a result of too much caffeine
- increased PMS symptoms in some women
- reduced fertility in some women
- increased risk of osteoporosis in postmenopausal women
- and in the most severe cases, caffeinism, which can cause high anxiety and bipolar schizophrenia, even psychosis

WHITE COFFEE CHEESECAKE
Makes 1 (9") cake

- 1 C. crushed vanilla wafer cookies
- 2 T. butter, melted
- 1 C. plus 3 T. sugar, divided
- 1 T. plus 1 tsp. cocoa powder, divided
- 4 (1 oz.) squares semi-sweet chocolate, grated
- 1 T. instant coffee granules
- 2 T. plus 1 tsp. coffee flavored liqueur, divided
- 4 (8 oz.) pkgs. cream cheese, softened
- 4 eggs
- 1 C. sour cream

Preheat oven to 350°. In a medium bowl, combine vanilla wafer cookie crumbs, melted butter, 1 tablespoon sugar and 1 tablespoon cocoa powder, mixing with a fork. Press mixture into the bottom of a 9" springform pan. Cover pan in aluminum foil and place in refrigerator while preparing the filling. To prepare filling, in a microwave-safe bowl or double boiler over medium heat, place grated chocolate. Heat until chocolate is completely melted, stirring occasionally. In a medium mixing bowl, beat cream cheese and 1 cup sugar at medium speed until well blended. In a small bowl, dissolve instant coffee granules in 2 tablespoons coffee liqueur. Add coffee mixture and melted chocolate to cream cheese mixture. Blend well and add eggs, one at a time, mixing well after each addition. Pour mixture over crust in pan. Place pan in a large baking pan and pour boiling water around pan until water reaches half way up sides of springform pan. Bake in oven for 1 hour. Remove springform pan from baking pan. Meanwhile, to make topping, in a medium bowl, combine sour cream, remaining 3 tablespoons sugar, remaining 1 teaspoon coffee liqueur and remaining 1 teaspoon cocoa powder. Mix well and spread over cheesecake. Return to oven for an additional 5 minutes. Remove from oven, cool and chill in refrigerator at least 5 hours or overnight before serving.

MOCHA LAYERED CAKE
Makes 1 (9″) cake

2¼ C. flour
1½ tsp. baking soda
1 C. plus 3 T. cocoa powder, divided
¾ C. strong brewed coffee, cold
¾ C. plus 3 T. coffee flavored liqueur

½ C. shortening
1 C. brown sugar
3 eggs, separated
¼ C. sugar
6 T. butter, softened
4 C. powdered sugar
2 T. hot brewed coffee

Preheat oven to 350°. Grease and lightly flour two 9″ round cake pans. Into a medium bowl, sift flour, baking soda and ½ cup cocoa powder and set aside. In a small bowl, combine ¾ cup cold coffee and ¾ cup coffee liqueur and set aside. In a large bowl, cream together shortening and brown sugar until lightened and fluffy. Beat in egg yolks, one at a time, mixing well. Alternating, stir in flour mixture and coffee mixture, beating well after each addition. In a medium mixing bowl, beat egg whites until soft peaks form and fold in sugar. Gently fold egg whites mixture into batter. Pour batter evenly into prepared pans. Bake in oven for 30 minutes, or until a toothpick inserted in center of cake comes out clean. Remove from oven and let cool for 10 minutes. Meanwhile, to prepare frosting, in a medium bowl, cream butter until fluffy. Fold in powdered sugar and remaining 3 tablespoons cocoa powder, remaining 3 tablespoons coffee liqueur and 2 tablespoons hot coffee. Mix well until frosting reaches desired consistency. To assemble cake, place one cake layer on a serving platter. Top with some of the frosting and the remaining cake layer. Spread remaining frosting over top and sides of cake.

COFFEE BUTTERCREAM CAKE

Makes 8 servings

15 egg whites, divided
3 C. sugar, divided
10 eggs, beaten
1¼ C. ground almonds
1¼ C. powdered sugar
1 C. pastry flour
1¼ C. plus 3 T. butter, divided

1³/₈ C. water, divided
Dash of coffee flavored extract
2½ C. heavy whipping cream
2½ C. semisweet chocolate, chopped
½ tsp. instant coffee granules

Preheat oven to 350°. Line two 10 x 15″ jellyroll pans with parchment paper. In a large bowl, beat 12 egg whites at high speed until stiff peaks form. Gradually fold in ¾ cup sugar. In a separate bowl, beat together 10 whole eggs, ground almonds, powdered sugar and flour, mixing until smooth. In a microwave-safe dish, melt 3 tablespoons butter in microwave and add to almond mixture. Fold in beaten egg whites and spread batter evenly into prepared jellyroll pans. Bake in oven for 10 minutes, or until a toothpick inserted in center of cakes comes out clean. Remove from oven and invert cakes onto wire racks to cool. Meanwhile, to prepare buttercream, in a small saucepan over medium heat, combine ³/₈ cup water and 1¼ cups sugar. Heat until mixture reaches between 234 and 240°F on a candy thermometer. While syrup is heating, in a medium mixing bowl, beat remaining 3 egg whites at medium speed. Increase speed to high and pour hot syrup into beaten egg whites. Continue beating until mixture cools to room temperature. Add remaining 1¼ cups butter and coffee extract, a little at a time, until mixture is smooth then set aside. To make ganache, in a small saucepan over medium heat, bring heavy cream to a boil. Add chopped chocolate and stir until chocolate is completely melted. Let mixture cool in refrigerator. To make syrup, in a separate small saucepan over medium heat, combine remaining 1 cup sugar and 1 cup water. Bring to a boil, reduce heat and let simmer for 1 minute. Stir in instant coffee granules. To assemble dessert, cut each cake in half (you will only use 3 of the halves). Place one cake layer on a serving platter and drizzle half of the coffee syrup. Spread half of the ganache over cake and top with another cake layer. Pour remaining syrup over layer and top with buttercream mixture. Place third cake layer on top and chill in refrigerator. Heat remaining ganache in a double boiler over medium heat. Place cooled cake on a wire rack and drizzle ganache over top, completely covering surface. Chill in refrigerator until firm. Before serving, trim sides of cake and cut into 8 servings.

FREEZER TIRAMISU
Makes 14 servings

½ C. strong brewed coffee
3 T. rum
2 (3 oz.) pkgs. ladyfingers
½ gallon coffee flavored ice cream, softened
4 (1 oz.) squares bitter-sweet chocolate, grated

1 (8 oz.) pkg. mascarpone cheese
3 T. coffee flavored liqueur
1 T. sugar
⅓ C. half n' half

In a medium bowl, combine coffee and rum and set aside. Line the inside of a large loaf pan with plastic wrap, letting plastic hang over edge. Line the bottom and sides of the pan with ladyfingers, rounded side out. Using a pastry brush, generously brush coffee mixture over ladyfingers. Set aside ½ cup of the grated chocolate. In a medium bowl, combine remaining grated chocolate and coffee flavored ice cream. Mix well and pour ice cream over ladyfingers in loaf pan, spreading evenly with a rubber spatula. Cover with plastic wrap and place in freezer for 2 hours or up to 5 days. Before serving, in a medium bowl, combine mascarpone cheese, coffee liqueur, sugar and half n' half, whisking until mixture has thickened. Remove dessert from pan by carefully lifting the plastic wrap. Invert tiramisu onto a serving platter and gently peel away the plastic wrap. Slice loaf into servings and drizzle cheese mixture over each serving. Sprinkle each serving with reserve grated chocolate.

"If I asked for a cup of coffee, someone would search for the double meaning."

Mae West

"*Coffee is the common man's gold, and like gold, it brings to every person the feeling of luxury and nobility.*"

Sheik Abdal-Kader

COST PER CUP
(when consumed at home)

Coffee	\$.05
Soft Drinks	\$.13
Milk	\$.16
Bottled Water	\$.25
Beer	\$.44
Table Wines	\$1.30

Green coffee, or unroasted coffee, is sold as a commodity on the world market. Therefore, the cost of coffee is affected by anything that alters the worldwide supply, such as freezing temperatures or drought. Even with the occasional price increase, coffee is very inexpensive when compared to other beverages consumed at home.

United States Bureau of Labor Statistics.
Division of Consumer Prices, May 1998, per eight fluid ounces.

COCONUT COFFEE TORTE
Makes 1 (9″) cake

1 (18¼ oz.) pkg. yellow
  cake mix
2½ tsp. instant coffee granules
½ C. coffee flavored liqueur,
  divided
2 C. milk

1 (5 oz.) pkg. instant vanilla
  pudding mix
1½ C. heavy whipping
  cream
3 T. sugar
3 C. shredded coconut

Preheat oven to 350°. Grease and lightly flour two 9″ cake
pans. In a large bowl, combine yellow cake mix and instant
coffee granules. Prepare cake mix according to package
directions and divide batter evenly into prepared cake
pans. Bake in oven according to package directions, remove and let cool on a wire rack. Using a serrated knife,
carefully cut each cake in half lengthwise to make 4 cake
layers. Sprinkle 1 tablespoon coffee liqueur over each of
the cake layers. In a medium bowl, prepare instant vanilla
pudding according to package directions, adding the re-

maining ¼ cup coffee liqueur. Spread ⅓ of the pudding mixture over three of the cake layers. Assemble cake by placing one cake layer on a serving platter. Top with ⅓ of the pudding mixture and another cake layer. Top with another ⅓ of the pudding mixture and a third layer. Top with remaining pudding mixture and final cake layer. In a medium mixing bowl, beat heavy cream until stiff peaks form and fold in sugar. Spread mixture over top and sides of torte and sprinkle top of cake with shredded coconut.

"Behind every successful woman, is a substantial amount of coffee."

Stephanie Piro

"Actually, this seems to be the basic need of the human heart in nearly every great crisis – a good hot cup of coffee."

Alexander King

CHOCOLATE CHIP COFFEE CRISPS

Makes 3 dozen

1 C. butter, softened
1 C. brown sugar
¾ C. sugar
2 eggs, beaten
3 T. coffee flavored liqueur

3 C. flour
¾ tsp. baking soda
¾ tsp. salt
1 tsp. cinnamon
3 C. milk chocolate chips

Preheat oven to 350°. Grease a baking sheet and set aside. In a large bowl, combine butter, brown sugar and sugar until lightened and fluffy. Add eggs, one at a time, beating well after each addition and stir in coffee liqueur. In a separate bowl, combine flour, baking soda, salt and cinnamon. Add flour mixture to butter mixture and stir until well combined. Drop dough by the tablespoonful onto prepared baking sheet. Bake in oven for 8 to 10 minutes. Remove from oven and let cool on a wire rack.

COFFEE ICE CREAM
Makes 8 to 10 servings

4 T. dark roast coffee
   grounds
2½ C. milk

1 C. brown sugar
6 egg yolks
2 C. heavy whipping cream

In a large bowl, place coffee grounds. In a medium sauce-pan over medium heat, place milk. Heat milk until almost boiling and pour hot milk over coffee. Set aside for 4 minutes. In a separate large bowl, using a wire whisk, beat together brown sugar and egg yolks. Pour mixture into coffee mixture, whisking constantly. Pour mixture back into medium saucepan through a fine hole sieve. Place saucepan over low heat and cook mixture for 1 to 2 minutes, until custard coats the back of a spoon, being careful not to boil. Pour mixture into a shallow freezer container and set aside to cool, stirring occasionally. Once cool, place mixture in freezer for 2 hours. After 2 hours, transfer mixture to a bowl and mix with a whisk until smooth. In a large mixing bowl, beat heavy cream until stiff peaks form. Fold whipped cream into frozen mixture and return to freezer for 1 additional hour, turn out into a bowl and whisk again. Return to freezer for an additional 3 to 4 hours, until mixture is frozen solid.

Note: If using an ice cream maker, do not whip the heavy cream. Instead, stir the cream into the coffee custard mixture before placing all in the ice cream machine.

BANANAS FOSTER WITH JAVA
Makes 4 to 6 servings

6 bananas
3 T. butter
¼ C. dark brown sugar

¼ C. strong brewed coffee
4 T. dark rum
Vanilla ice cream

Peel the bananas and cut each banana in half lengthwise. In a large saucepan over medium heat, place butter. Heat until butter is melted and add the banana slices. Cook bananas for 3 minutes, flipping once. Sprinkle brown sugar generously over bananas and pour brewed coffee over bananas. Continue to heat for 2 to 3 minutes, stirring occasionally, until bananas are tender. Add rum and bring mixture to a boil. With a long match, ignite the rum in the pan, letting the mixture burn until the flames subside. Carefully place banana slices on serving plates and spoon sauce over bananas. Serve with a small scoop of vanilla ice cream.

> *"How sweet coffee tastes! Lovlier than a thousand kisses, sweeter than Muscatel wine!"*
>
> **Johann Sebastian Bach**

"*The morning cup of coffee has an exhilaration about it which the cheering influence of the afternoon or evening cup of tea cannot be expected to reproduce.*"

Oliver Wendall Holmes, Sr.

COFFEE COOKIES

Makes about 2 dozen

½ C. shortening
⅔ C. sugar
2 T. instant coffee granules
1 egg, beaten

¾ C. flour
½ tsp. vanilla
½ C. chopped walnuts

Preheat oven to 350°. Grease a baking sheet and set aside. In a medium bowl, cream together shortening, sugar and instant coffee granules. Stir in beaten egg, flour, vanilla and chopped nuts. Mix until well combined and drop cookies by the teaspoonful onto prepared baking sheet. Bake in oven for 10 to 12 minutes, or until edges of cookies are golden brown. Remove from oven and let cool on a wire rack.

COFFEE LINGO

If you've ever wandered into a coffee shop and heard the barista yell out, "Short Skinny Latte No Whip," you might be wondering just what all the coffee lingo means. Here is a simple guide to help you decipher those secret code words.

Addshot: add an extra shot of espresso

Americano: espresso diluted with hot water; also known as Café Americano

Barista: espresso bartender

Breve: espresso with half n' half or skimmed milk; short for Espresso Breve

Café Au Lait: coffee served French style poured simultaneously with boiled milk into the cup

Café Crème: 1½ ounces espresso with 1 ounce heavy cream; also known as Espresso Crème

Café Latte: espresso made with steamed milk and topped with foamed milk; also known simply as Latte

Café Macchiato: espresso marked, or stained, with a dollop of foamed milk

Café Mocha: a latte with chocolate; also known simply as Mocha

Cappuccino: a shot of espresso with foamed milk
  ladled on top

Demitasse: a small cup for serving espresso straight

Double Double: double cream, double sugar;
  also known as Cake in a Cup

Frappuccino: a blended coffee drink combining
  coffee, milk, sugar, ice and other ingredients;
  originally developed by Starbucks

Grande: 16 ounce cup

Half-Caf: Half decaf

No Whip: No whipped topping; the term Whipless
  is also used

On a Leash: Ordered to go; the term With Handles
  is also used

Short: 8 ounce cup

Shot: approximately ¾ to 1 ounce espresso;
  one Shot is known as a Single

Shot in the Dark: a regular coffee with a shot
  of espresso; also known as a Speed Ball

Skinny: a latte made with nonfat or skimmed milk

Tall: 12 ounce cup; also known as a Regular

Venti: 20 ounce cup; a 24 ounce cup is used
  for a Venti cold drink

Zebra: half regular mocha and half white mocha

CARAMEL TASSIES
Makes 2 dozen

1 (8 oz.) pkg. cream
cheese, softened
2 C. flour
1½ C. shortening, divided
1 (14 oz.) pkg. individual
caramels, unwrapped
2 (5 oz.) cans evaporated

milk, divided
4 tsp. coffee flavored
liqueur, divided
½ C. butter, softened
⅔ C. sugar
¼ C. finely ground
pecans, optional

Preheat oven to 350°. In a medium bowl, combine cream cheese, flour and 1 cup shortening. Mix well and divide mixture evenly into 12 mini muffin cups, pressing dough into bottom of cups. Bake in oven for 18 minutes. In a microwave-safe bowl, place unwrapped caramels. Heat in microwave until caramels are melted, stirring after every 30 seconds. Add 1 can evaporated milk and 2 teaspoons coffee liqueur, mixing well. Set mixture aside to thicken. In a medium mixing bowl, combine butter, remaining ½ cup shortening, remaining 1 can evaporated milk, remaining 2 teaspoons coffee liqueur and sugar at medium low speed for 8 minutes. Fill each muffin cup halfway with caramel. Let sit for 10 minutes and sprinkle topping mixture over caramel in each muffin cup. If desired, sprinkle ground pecans over topping mixture.

> *"Sleep is a symptom of caffeine deprivation."*
>
> **Author Unknown**

JAVA BARS
Makes 12 to 16 servings

¾ C. butter, softened, divided
½ C. sugar
1 tsp. vanilla
1 egg
2 C. graham cracker crumbs
½ C. finely chopped walnuts
¾ C. shredded coconut

2 tsp. instant coffee granules
2 T. strong brewed coffee
2 1/2 C. powdered sugar
¼ C. cocoa powder
2 T. milk
6 (1 oz.) squares white chocolate

Grease a 9 x 13″ baking dish and set aside. In a double boiler over low heat, combine ½ cup butter, sugar, vanilla and egg. Heat, stirring frequently, until mixture is thickened. Stir in graham cracker crumbs, shredded coconut and finely chopped walnuts. Mix well and pour mixture into prepared baking dish and let cool. To prepare filling, in a medium bowl, combine instant coffee granules and coffee, stirring until coffee granules are completely dissolved.

Mix in powdered sugar, cocoa powder, remaining ¼ cup butter and milk. Spread filling mixture over layer in baking dish and chill in refrigerator for 15 minutes. Meanwhile, to make topping, in a double boiler over low heat, melt white chocolate squares, stirring frequently, until smooth. Drizzle melted white chocolate over layers in pan. Chill in refrigerator. Before serving, cut into bars.

DARK COFFEE & CHOCOLATE MOUSSE CAKE

Makes 8 servings

4 eggs
1 C. sugar, divided
²/₃ C. flour, sifted
¼ C. cocoa powder, sifted
2 T. dark roast coffee grounds

¼ C. coffee flavored liqueur
1½ C. heavy whipping cream, divided
4 egg yolks
Powdered sugar

Preheat oven to 350°. Grease an 8″ square baking dish and a 9″ round cake pan. In a double boiler over medium heat, place 4 eggs and ½ cup sugar. Heat, whisking constantly, until thickened. Gently mix in sifted flour and cocoa powder. Pour ¹/₃ of the batter into the square baking dish and pour the remaining batter into the round cake pan. Bake square cake in oven for 15 minutes and round cake for 30 minutes, until a toothpick inserted in center of cakes comes out clean. Remove from oven and let cool. Remove round cake from pan and slice in half lengthwise to make two rounds. Place one round back in the bottom of the round cake pan. Trim the edges of the square cake and cut into 4 equal rectangles and line the sides of the round pan with the rectangles. To prepare mousse filling, in a medium bowl, place coffee grounds. In a microwave-safe measuring cup, place ¾ cup heavy cream. Heat in microwave until cream is almost boiling and pour over coffee grounds in bowl. Let set for 4 minutes and pour mixture through a fine hole sieve into a separate bowl. In a medium saucepan, combine remaining ½ cup sugar and ½ cup water. Bring to a low boil, stirring constantly, until mixture thickens to a syrup. Remove from heat and let cool for 5 minutes. Place egg yolks in a separate bowl and pour syrup mixture over egg yolks, whisking thoroughly until mixture is very thick. In a large mixing bowl, place remaining ¾ cup heavy cream. Add coffee cream mixture and beat at high speed until soft peaks form. Fold egg mixture into cream mixture and pour over cake layer in cake pan. Place in freezer for 20 minutes. Sprinkle coffee liqueur over remaining round cake layer and place on top of mousse filling in pan. Cover and return to freezer for an additional 4 hours. Remove from freezer and, before serving, dust with powdered sugar.

CAPPUCCINO TORTE

Makes 6 to 8 servings

6 T. butter, melted
1¼ C. crushed shortbread cookies
¼ tsp. cinnamon
1½ T. unflavored gelatin
3 T. cold water
2 eggs, separated

½ C. brown sugar
4 (1 oz.) square semisweet chocolate, chopped
¾ C. hot strong brewed coffee or espresso
1⅔ C. heavy whipping cream, divided

In a medium bowl, combine melted butter, crushed short-bread and cinnamon. Mix well and pour mixture into a greased 8″ springform pan. Chill layer in refrigerator while preparing filling. To make filling, in a medium bowl, place cold water. Sprinkle gelatin over water and set aside for 5 minutes. Place a pan filled with water over medium high heat. Set bowl over hot water and stir gelatin mixture until gelatin is completely dissolved. In a separate bowl, using a wire whisk, combine egg yolks and brown sugar, whisking until thickened. In a medium saucepan, combine chopped chocolate and hot coffee or espresso, stirring until chocolate is completely melted. Place saucepan over medium low heat and add egg yolk mixture, cooking for 1 to 2 minutes, until thickened. Stir in gelatin mixture. Set aside until mixture begins to set, stirring occasionally. In a medium mixing bowl, beat $2/3$ cup heavy cream until soft peaks form. Whisk in the egg whites and beat until stiff peaks form. Fold the cream mixture into the coffee mixture and pour over layer in springform pan. Return to refrigerator for 2 hours. Before serving, whip remaining 1 cup heavy cream until stiff peaks form. Cut torte into wedges and serve each with a dollop of whipped cream.

COFFEE CREPES
Makes 6 servings

²/₃ C. flour
¼ C. buckwheat flour
¼ tsp. salt
1 egg, beaten

1 C. milk, divided
1 T. butter, melted
½ C. strong brewed coffee
Oil for frying

Into a large mixing bowl, sift the flour, buckwheat flour and salt. Make a well in the center of the dry mixture and add the beaten egg, ½ cup milk and melted butter. Beat at low speed until smooth and gradually add remaining ½ cup milk and brewed coffee. Meanwhile, in a small saucepan or 8″ crepe pan over high heat, place a thin drizzle of oil. When oil is hot, pour enough batter to just barely cover the bottom of the pan. Cook for 2 to 3 minutes, until bottom side is golden brown. Carefully flip over by running a thin spatula or knife under the crepe and turning fully on un-cooked side. Heat for an additional 1 to 2 minutes, until remaining side of crepe is golden brown. Serve crepes with various fillings, such as fresh cut fruit, whipped topping, flavored butter or cream filling.

"*I believe humans get a lot done, not because we're smart, but because we have thumbs so we can make coffee.*"

Flash Rosenberg

SOUFFLÉ CAFÉ
Makes 10 servings

1½ C. brewed coffee
½ C. milk
½ C. sugar, divided
¼ tsp. salt, divided
1 (1 oz.) env. unflavored
  gelatin

3 eggs, separated
½ tsp. vanilla
Whipped topping, optional
Coffee beans, optional

In a double boiler over medium heat, combine coffee, milk, ¼ cup sugar, ⅛ teaspoon salt and gelatin. Heat, stirring frequently, until sugar, salt and gelatin are dissolved. Stir in remaining ¼ cup sugar, remaining ⅛ teaspoon salt and egg yolks. Continue to cook, stirring occasionally, until mixture is thickened and coats the back of a metal spoon. Remove from heat and let cool slightly. In a medium mixing bowl, beat egg whites until stiff peaks form. Fold egg whites and vanilla into coffee mixture. Pour mixture into a serving dish or mold and chill in refrigerator until set. Before serving, invert soufflé onto a serving dish and, if desired, garnish with whipped topping and coffee beans.

"Strong coffee, much strong
coffee, is what awakens me.
Coffee gives me warmth,
waking, an unusual force
and a pain that is
not without great plesure."

Napoleon Bonaparte

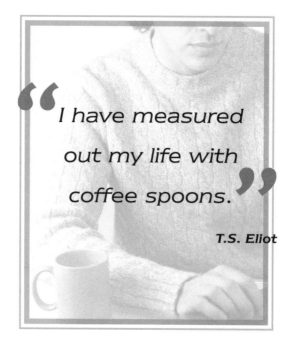

"I have measured out my life with coffee spoons."

T.S. Eliot

SIMPLE COFFEE MOUSSE
WITH COCONUT

Makes 3 cups

2 T. coffee flavored liqueur
¼ C. shredded coconut
1 (8 oz.) container frozen
  whipped topping, thawed

Sprigs of fresh mint
  for garnish

In a medium bowl, fold coffee liqueur and shredded coconut into whipped topping, mixing until well combined. Pour mixture into an 8˝ square baking dish and place in freezer for 4 hours, or until firm. To serve, spoon mixture into martini glasses and garnish with sprigs of fresh mint.

THE ROAST

You may have noticed that the coffee you can purchase in stores is available in many different roasts. The different roasts can determine the color, flavor and strength of the beans. Roasting brings the delicate coffee from within each bean to the surface, giving coffee its distinctive aroma and taste. As soon as the beans are roasted, they begin to lose flavor and aroma, so it is best to purchase coffee beans as close to the roasting date as possible. Grinding the beans at home, or at the store, is a great way to release additional flavor from the beans.

TYPICAL COFFEE ROASTS

Cinnamon – the beans are light brown and there is no visible oil. There is a baked or bread taste, like toasted grain.

New England – a term popular in the eastern United States. The beans are a little darker than cinnamon roast, without the grainy flavor.

Light Roast – the beans are cinnamon brown and have higher acidity than dark roasts and a less bitter taste.

Medium or Straight Roast – the flavor is a bit more noticeable than light roast and the beans are a chestnut brown color.

Full City – medium, dark brown beans with a slight caramel or chocolate taste. The beans will show some oil on the surface.

Dark or High Roast – the beans are nearly black and develop a slightly bitter flavor.

Continental or Vienna Roast – the lightest of the very dark roasts.

French Roast – the beans are black and an oil emerges on the surface of the beans.

French Sugar Roast – sugar is added during roasting, which caramelizes to make a shiny, oily black bean with a bitter flavor.

New Orleans Roast – between a French and Espresso roast in darkness.

Italian or Espresso Roast – the roast is dark and almost burned with a strong, bitter flavor. Excellent when used in espresso machines.

Turkish Roast – the beans are almost burned, as this is one of the darkest roasts available. (Also known as Arabian, Balkan Greek, Cuban, Iranian and Lebanese Roast.)

MACADAMIA MUFFINS
Makes 12 servings

1½ T. coffee grounds
1 C. milk
4 T. butter
1 egg, slightly beaten

2½ C. flour
2 tsp. baking powder
10 T. muscovado sugar*
½ C. macadamia nuts

Preheat oven to 400°. Lightly grease 12 muffin cups and set aside. In a large bowl, place coffee grounds. In a medium saucepan over medium heat, place milk. Heat milk until almost boiling and pour hot milk over coffee. Set aside for 4 minutes. Pour mixture back into bowl through a fine hole sieve. Add butter and stir until butter is completely melted. Set aside until mixture cools and stir in beaten egg. Into a separate bowl, sift flour and baking powder. Stir in sugar and macadamia nuts. Add flour mixture to coffee mixture and stir until just combined, being careful not to overmix. Divide mixture evenly into muffin cups and bake in oven for 15 minutes, or until firm in the center. Remove from oven and let muffins cool on a wire rack.

*Muscovado sugar is a specialty sugar that is moist
and brown in color.

Coffee should be black as hell, strong as death, and as sweet as love.

Turkish Proverb

> "Making coffee has become the great compromise of the decade. It's the only thing real men do that doesn't seem to threaten their masculinity. To women, it's on the same domestic entry level as putting the spring back into the toilet-tissue holder or taking a chicken out of the freezer to thaw."

Erma Bombeck

ESPRESSO GRANITA

Makes 6 servings

½ C. sugar
2½ C. hot strong brewed
 coffee or espresso

Whipped topping, optional

In a medium bowl, combine sugar and hot coffee or espresso, mixing until sugar is completely dissolved. Set aside to cool and pour into a shallow freezer container. Place mixture in freezer for 3 hours, or until ice crystals begin to form at the edge of the container. Grate mixture with a fork until rough in texture and return to freezer for 1 additional hour. Again, grate with a fork and return to freezer. Repeat process until mixture is completely frozen. Before serving, break up mixture once again with a fork and scoop into glasses. If desired, garnish with whipped topping before serving.

CUP O' JOE BISCOTTI
Makes about 30 servings

⅓ C. espresso roast
   coffee beans
⅔ C. blanched almonds
2 C. flour
1½ tsp. baking powder
¼ tsp. salt

6 T. butter, cut into pieces
¾ C. sugar
2 eggs, beaten
1½ T. strong brewed coffee
1 tsp. cinnamon

Preheat oven to 350°. On a large baking sheet, place coffee beans on one half and blanched almonds on the other half. Roast in oven for 10 minutes, remove and let cool. In a blender or coffee grinder, place coffee beans and process until finely ground and set aside. Repeat with almonds and set aside. Into a medium bowl, sift flour, baking powder and salt. Using a pastry blender, cut in butter until mixture resembles breadcrumbs. Stir in sugar, ground coffee beans and ground almonds. Stir in beaten eggs and enough brewed coffee to form a fairly firm dough. Mix well and lightly knead dough until smooth. Divide dough in half and shape each half into a log about 3″ in diameter. Place logs on a greased baking sheet and dust with cinnamon. Bake in oven for 20 minutes. Remove from oven and, using a serrated knife, cut logs into 1½″ thick slices. Place slices on their sides on a baking sheet and return to oven for an additional 10 minutes, or until lightly browned. Remove and let cool on a wire rack. Serve biscotti with a warm cup o' joe!

" *I think if I were a woman,*

I'd wear coffee as a perfume. "

John Van Druten

CAFÉ CHILI WITH WASABI
Makes 8 servings

4 T. vegetable oil, divided	1 T. ground cumin
2 onions, chopped	¼ C. brown sugar
4 cloves garlic, minced	1 tsp. oregano
1 lb. ground beef	1 tsp. cayenne pepper
¾ lb. spicy Italian sausage	1 tsp. coriander
1 (14½ oz.) can diced to-matoes in juice	1 tsp. salt
1 (12 oz.) can dark beer	1 T. wasabi paste
1 C. strong brewed coffee	3 (15 oz.) can kidney beans, divided
2 (6 oz.) cans tomato paste	2 chile peppers, chopped
1 (14 oz.) can beef broth	1 Serrano pepper, chopped
¼ C. chili powder	1 habanero pepper, sliced

In a large pot over medium heat, place 2 tablespoons oil. Add chopped onions, minced garlic, ground beef and ground sausage and sauté until meats are cooked throughout and onions are transparent. Add diced tomatoes in juice, beer, coffee, tomato paste and beef broth. Mix well and stir in chili powder, cumin, brown sugar, oregano, cayenne pepper, coriander, salt and wasabi paste. Add one can kidney beans and bring chili to a boil. Reduce heat, cover and let simmer. Meanwhile, in a large skillet over medium heat, place remaining 2 tablespoons oil. Add chopped chile peppers, chopped Serrano pepper and sliced habanero pepper. Sauté for 5 to 10 minutes, until just tender and add to remaining ingredients in pot. Let simmer for 2 hours. Stir in remaining 2 cans of kidney beans and heat for an additional 45 minutes.

COFFEE STORAGE

GREEN COFFEE

Coffee that has not been roasted, otherwise known as green coffee, is the easiest to store. Green coffee can last for more than one year when stored in an tightly sealed airtight container in a cool place. However, the green coffee beans still need to be roasted before making coffee.

WHOLE COFFEE BEANS

Roasted whole coffee beans will last for 1 to 2 weeks when stored in an airtight container at room temperature. If you are unable to use the coffee beans within 2 weeks, they can be frozen when wrapped in several layers of plastic or in an airtight container or bag with as much air released as possible. The beans do not need to be thawed before grinding. Do not store coffee in the refrigerator, as it will pick up flavors and odors from other foods.

GROUND COFFEE

Only buy as much ground coffee as you can use up quickly, as it will go stale in just a few days. Store ground coffee in an airtight, light-proof container at room temperature.

INDEX

Bananas Foster with Java 86

Benefits.. 68

Black Russian Cake.. 58

Café Chili with Wasabi 114

Café Mudslide.. 39

Café Yogurt 18

Caffeine... 67

Calypso Coffee 17

Cappuccino Cheesecake 56

Cappuccino Torte 98

Caramel Tassies 92

Chilled Mocha Fusion 16

Chocolate Buzz 9

Chocolate Chip Coffee Crisps 83

Cinnamon Hazelnut Coffee............................. 12

Coconut Coffee Torte....................................... 80

C O F F E E

Coffea Arabica.. 6

Coffea Canephora 7

Coffee Bean 6

Coffee Buttercream Cake 74

Coffee Cookies 89

Coffee Crepes 100

Coffee Ice Cream 84

Coffee Ice Cream Pie 64

Coffee Producing Countries............................ 42

Cold Café Latte 23

Cost per Cup 79

Crème Brulee 52

Cup o' Joe Biscotti 112

Dark Coffee & Chocolate Mousse Cake 96

Decaf 67

Dreamy Mocha Cake 60

Espresso Granita 111

Fertilizer 24

Fireside Coffee 26